M *marsh mask milkweed mist moon mosquito moth mouse mouth mushrooms*

N *naked nasturtium navel nest net nightingale nixie nose nuts*

O *oak ocean on orange owl*

P *pack paddle pan peaks pear perch percolator pie pineapple pinecone pine trees plaid plum pond porcupine*

Q *queen Queen Anne's lace quilt quince*

R *rabbit race rain raincoat ribbon roller skates roses*

S *sail sand sandal scallop sea seagull sea urchin seaweed shell sit spine starfish stick sun sunglasses swimsuit*

T *table tablecloth tail talk teacup teapot teeth telephones thread ties toe top topknots tulips turtle twins twist two*

U *umbrella uncombed under underwear upon ups-a-daisies*

V *valentine valley vegetables vest village violets violin*

W *wade water water lily weather vane weeds wheel wheelbarrow whistle wind windmill wings wood wren*

X *xxx*

Y *yarn yarrow yawn yellow jackets Yorkshire terrier*

Z *zinnia zipper zoo*

A
LITTLE
ALPHABET

A LITTLE ALPHABET

BY
TRINA SCHART HYMAN

BOOKS OF WONDER
WILLIAM MORROW & COMPANY
NEW YORK

Pen and ink and watercolors were used for the full-color art.
Copyright © 1980, 1993 by Trina Schart Hyman
Originally published in two colors by Little, Brown and Company,
Boston, 1980.
All rights reserved.
No part of this book may be reproduced or utilized in any form or by any
means, electronic or mechanical, including photocopying, recording, or by any
information storage and retrieval system, without permission in writing from
the Publisher. Inquiries should be addressed to
William Morrow and Company, Inc.,
1350 Avenue of the Americas, New York, NY 10019 or
Books of Wonder, 132 Seventh Avenue at 18th Street, New York, NY 10011.
Printed in the United States of America.
1 2 3 4 5 6 7 8 9 10
Library of Congress Cataloging-in-Publication Data
Hyman, Trina Schart. A little alphabet / by Trina Schart Hyman. p.   cm. —
(Books of wonder) Originally published: Boston : Little, Brown, c1980.
Summary: Each letter of the alphabet is illustrated with a boy or girl playing
with or using objects beginning with that letter.
ISBN 0-688-12035-0 (LE)
1. English language—Alphabet—Juvenile literature. [1. Alphabet.]
I. Title. II. Series. PE1155.H9 1993 421′.1—dc20 [E]
92-29692 CIP AC

Books of Wonder is a registered trademark of Ozma, Inc.

To
John Grandits
with affection
and gratitude
T.S.H.